OLSAT® Practice Test for Pre-Kindergarten and Kindergarten

Illustrations by: Mirona Jova
Written and published by: Bright Kids NYC

Copyright © 2010 by Bright Kids NYC Inc. All of the questions in this book have been created by the staff and consultants of Bright Kids NYC Inc.

The Otis-Lennon School Ability Test (OLSAT®) is a registered trademark of NCS Pearson Inc. Pearson Inc. neither endorses nor supports the content of the OLSAT® Practice Test.

All rights reserved. No part of this book may be reproduced or transmitted in any form or by any means without written permission from the author. ISBN (978-0-9840810-8-0)

Corporate Headquarters:
Bright Kids NYC
225 Broadway, Suite 1504
New York, NY 10007
www.brightkidsnyc.com
info@brightkidsnyc.com
917-539-4575

Table of Contents

OLSAT® Practice Test for Pre-K and Kindergarten

Bright Kids NYC Inc. ©

About Bright Kids NYC

Bright Kids NYC was founded in New York City to provide language arts and math enrichment for young children and to educate parents about standardized tests through workshops and consultations, as well as to prepare young children for such tests through assessments, tutoring and publications. Our philosophy is that regardless of age, test-taking is a skill than can be acquired and mastered through practice.

At Bright Kids NYC, we strive to provide the best learning materials. Our publications are truly unique. First, all of our books have been created by qualified psychologists, learning specialists and teachers. Second, our books have been tested by hundreds of children in our tutoring practice. Since children can make associations that many adults cannot, testing of materials by children is critical to creating successful test preparation guides. Finally, our learning specialists and teaching staff have provided practical strategies and tips so parents can best help their child prepare to compete successfully on standardized tests.

Feel free to contact us should you have any questions or concerns.

Corporate Headquarters:
Bright Kids NYC
225 Broadway, Suite 1504
New York, NY 10007
www.brightkidsnyc.com
info@brightkidsnyc.com
917-539-4575

OLSAT® Practice Test for Pre-K and Kindergarten

Bright Kids NYC Inc. ©

Introduction

Bright Kids NYC created the OLSAT® Practice Test to familiarize children with the content and the format of the OLSAT®. Children, no matter how bright they are, do not always perform well when they are not accustomed to the format and the structure of a test. Children can misunderstand the directions, fail to look at all the answer choices, and may not always listen carefully to the questions. Thus, without adequate preparation and familiarization, children may not always perform to the best of their ability on standardized tests such as the OLSAT®.

The Bright Kids NYC OLSAT® Practice Test for Pre-Kindergarten and Kindergarten can be used either as a diagnostic to assess your child's abilities or can be administered after working though our OLSAT® Practice Test to see how your child would potentially perform on a simulated OLSAT® test.

This Bright Kids NYC OLSAT® Practice Test is not designed to generate a score or a percentile rank as the test has not been standardized with the actual OLSAT® norms and standards. The objective of the practice test is to identify your child's strengths and weaknesses and test-taking ability so that you can prepare your child adequately for the actual test. The Answer Key includes the question type so that you can easily identify what type of OLSAT® questions your child is struggling with.

In order to maximize the effectiveness of the Bright Kids NYC OLSAT® Practice Test, it is important to first familiarize yourself with the test and its instructions. In addition, it is recommended that you designate a quiet place to work with your child, ideally in a neutral environment free of noise and clutter. Finally, provide a comfortable and a proper seating arrangement to enable your child to focus and concentrate to the best of his or her ability.

Children will be taking many standardized tests throughout their school years. Teaching your child critical thinking skills along with test-taking strategies at a young age will benefit your child for many years to come. Our philosophy is that regardless of age, test-taking is a skill than can be acquired and mastered through practice.

OLSAT® Practice Test for Pre-K and Kindergarten

Bright Kids NYC Inc. ©

OLSAT® Overview

The Otis-Lennon School Ability Test® (OLSAT®) was created and published by Dr. Arthur Otis at Stanford University in 1918.. The Otis Group Intelligence Scale was followed by the Otis Self-Administering Tests of Mental Ability, the Otis Quick-Scoring Mental Ability Tests, the Otis-Lennon Mental Ability Test, and finally the Otis-Lennon School Ability Test. As the years went by, the term "mental ability" was changed to "school ability". The purpose of the test is to assess examinees' ability to cope with school learning tasks, to suggest their possible placement for school learning functions, and to evaluate their achievement in school learning tasks.

The latest version of the Otis Lennon School Ability Test® is the Eighth Edition (OLSAT® 8), which is administered in various education programs in the country such as New York, Connecticut, California, Texas, and Virginia. Some of these programs are described below.

New York City Gifted and Talented Programs administer the OLSAT® for entry into District and Citywide Gifted and Talented Programs. The OLSAT® is administered in conjunction with the Naglieri Nonverbal Ability Test (NNAT®2). Currently, students are required to perform at or above the 90th percentile rank to be eligible for the District Programs and at or above the 97th percentile rank to be eligible for the Citywide Programs. Additional information can be found at http://schools.nyc.gov/Academics/GiftedandTalented.

The Davis Unified School District in California uses the OLSAT® for students in Grades 3-8 to qualify for entry into the District Gifted and Talented Programs. Students must receive a total OLSAT® score of 96% or higher and a Verbal or Nonverbal score in the 96th percentile or higher to qualify for the Gifted and Talented Education Programs (GATE).

The Greenwich Public Schools District Board of Education uses the OLSAT®, in conjunction with the Stanford Achievement Test, to evaluate children in 3rd, 5th, and 7th grades, to measure accountability. Each student's OLSAT® score helps predict his or her performance on the Stanford Achievement Test (SAT), and enables District to compare achievement scores. The OLSAT® is also used to predict performance on the Connecticut Mastery Test, a mandated year-end exam.

Bright Kids NYC Inc. ©

Content of Pre-Kindergarten (Pre-K) and Kindergarten Test (Level A)

In order to succeed on the OLSAT®, students must perceive accurately and recall what has been perceived, understand patterns and relationships, reason abstract items, and apply generalizations to contexts both new and different. These capabilities are measured through performance on classifications, analogies, following directions, aural reasoning, figural and pictorial sequencing, matrix completion, and arithmetic reasoning for Pre-K and Kindergarten children.

Verbal Reasoning

Verbal skills are centered on a child's ability to listen carefully, follow directions, and understand vocabulary through receptive language. While verbal sections do require verbal knowledge, all multiple choice options are given in a visual form. Children must select an answer based on listening, inferences, and background knowledge of both words and pictures.

There are three types of questions used to test verbal skills:

1. **Following Directions:** Following directions questions assess a child's ability to select a representation that corresponds to a verbal description that is read out loud. Children are asked to apply relational concepts when finding the correct answer to pictorial and figural representations .

2. **Aural Reasoning:** Aural reasoning questions test the ability to visualize a situation, integrate appropriate details, and synthesize what has been described. Children are asked to understand details, understand main ideas, and predict outcomes of situations.

3. **Arithmetic Reasoning:** Arithmetic reasoning incorporates number reasoning into the solving of verbal problems. This section tests basic mathematical reasoning concepts such as counting, quantity, estimation, and inequalities as well as more complex reasoning skills requiring children to solve basic word problems involving addition, subtraction, and simple fractions.

Nonverbal Reasoning

Nonverbal skills focus on a child's visual, spatial, and arithmetic understandings. Unlike the verbal sections, no verbal background knowledge is needed in this section. These nonverbal sections highlight reasoning skills independent of language (with the exception of the test directions which give verbal instructions on how to complete the tasks).

There are four types of questions which are used to practice nonverbal skills:

1. **Analogies:** An analogy is defined as reasoning or explaining from parallel cases. In other words, an analogy is a comparison between two different things that highlight some point of similarity. For children, analogical reasoning is assessed through pictures or figural elements. Analogy questions require children to infer a relationship between the first two items and then select an item that completes the second relationship in the same way. Analogies can be figural—which represents geometric shapes—or pictorial.

2. **Classifications:** Classifications require children to figure out what does not belong among a group of items. All but one of the pictures or figures in each question share a minimum of one common trait or characteristic, requiring the child to evaluate similarities and differences among each in order to select the item that does not belong. Classifications can be figural—which represents geometric shapes—or pictorial.

3. **Series:** Picture or Figural Series assess the ability to evaluate a sequential series of pictures or geometric shapes and then predict the next occurrence, or simply "what comes next".

4. **Pattern Matrices:** Pattern Matrices evaluate the ability to find the next step in a geometric series based on a set of rules. Children need to understand the rule and predict what shape would come next by applying the same rule.

OLSAT® Test Structure

The OLSAT® is a multiple choice test. It is not necessary for children to know how to read or write to take the Pre-K or Kindergarten test. The Pre-K test is administered one-on-one, while the Kindergarten test is administered in a group. Pre-K children are not required to mark or bubble their answers; they can simply point to the answer which in turn will be recorded by the administrator.

The OLSAT® content and structure varies for each entry level. For Pre-K and Kindergarten children in New York City, the same level test (Level A) is utilized. The Kindergarten Entry test (Pre-K test) is 40 questions and the First Grade Entry test (Kindergarten test) has an additional 20 questions for a total of 60 questions.

In most other parts of the country, the OLSAT® is typically taken when children are at least four and a half years old and are already in Kindergarten. These children must answer all 60 questions on the Level A test in a group setting. Children in First and Second Grade take the Level B and Level C tests respectively.

TABLE 1: Distribution of Types of Questions[1]

Subtest	Pre-Kindergarten	Kindergarten
VERBAL		
Following Directions	6	14
Aural Reasoning	5	9
Arithmetic Reasoning	3	6
NONVERBAL		
Picture Classifications	7	7
Figural Classifications	5	5
Picture Analogies	5	5
Figural Analogies	7	7
Picture Series	1	3
Figural Series	0	1
Pattern Matrices	1	3
Total	**40**	**60**

[1] This may or may not represent the question mix of the actual OLSAT® test, as the mix between verbal and nonverbal questions and among different types of questions may change from year to year.

Bright Kids NYC Inc. ©

Scoring Guidelines

When it comes to the results of the OLSAT® test, it comprises a wealth of useful information for test users. Derived scores based on age comparisons and derived scores based on grade comparisons can be provided for Total, Verbal, and Nonverbal raw scores. Raw score, which is defined as the number of questions answered correctly, does not provide enough information about the level of quality of student performance. On the other hand, the scaled score system connects all test levels and yields a continuous scale that can be used to compare the performance of students taking different levels of the same content cluster. Scaled scores are especially useful for comparing results from the same content cluster across levels, for evaluating changes in performance over time, and for out-of-level testing. Scaled scores can also be translated into percentile ranks.

For example, New York City Gifted and Talented Programs only provide percentile ranks for the overall combined score, while other districts in the US provide more detailed information. Since the test changes from year to year, the number of questions a child can answer correctly to obtain a specific scaled score will vary based on that particular test's curve and distribution.

The Bright Kids NYC OLSAT® Practice Test can be scored only based on total number of correct answers, or the overall raw score. Since this practice test has not been standardized with the OLSAT®, scaled scores or percentile ranks cannot be obtained from the raw score. Please realize that a child can miss many questions on the test and still obtain a high score. Thus, it is important that this practice test is utilized as a learning tool to help evaluate a child's strengths and weaknesses rather than to estimate a scaled score or a percentile rank.

General Administration Guidelines

For Pre-Kindergarten

The test is typically administered in three parts and in one sitting. There is a five minute recommended rest period between parts one and two and two rest periods in part three. The test pace is determined by the examiner, so there is no specific time limit for each part. The time allocations are shown to determine how much time is needed to complete the test. The recommended timeline is as follows:

Part 1 Examples	Approximately 8-10 minutes
Part 1 Administration	Approximately 6-8 minutes
Rest Period	**Approximately 5 minutes**
Part 2 Examples	Approximately 8-10 minutes
Part 2 Administration	Approximately 6-8 minutes
Rest Period	**Approximately 5 minutes**
Part 3 Examples	Approximately 8-10 minutes
Part 3 Administration (items 25-40)	Approximately 10-12 minutes

For Kindergarten

Part 1 and Part 2 and questions 25-40 of Part 3 are administered in the same way.

Rest Period	**Approximately 5 minutes**
Part 3 Administration (items 41-60)	Approximately 15-20 minutes

Getting Ready

Materials

1. A stapled copy of the test questions that are removed from this book. Also detach the Answer Key if your child is in Pre-Kindergarten so that you can record the answers.

2. Several No. 2 soft lead pencils, erasers, and pencil sharpeners for Kindergarten students.

3. Ideally, a "Do Not Disturb" sign for the room where you will be administering the test.

Prior to Testing

1. Familiarize yourself with the test and the instructions. Take the actual test to make sure that you can later explain to the child why certain answers are correct or incorrect.

2. Provide satisfactory physical conditions in the room where the child will be taking the test. Make sure that there is ample lighting and ventilation. Make sure that the table is clutter free and that the child and you can both sit comfortably at the table together.

3. To prevent interruptions, give the child the test when there are no other distractions in the house. If the house is not suitable, try to find a local library or a school.

During Testing

1. If the child is in Kindergarten, make sure that he or she is comfortable filling in the answers. Help the child to make sure that they know how to accurately mark the answers.

2. Read all instructions exactly as they are written; do not paraphrase or change the questions.

3. Read each item only once unless there were other disturbances in the room.

4. Pace the test and utilize the breaks as needed. Young children, particularly Pre-Kindergarten students, often need breaks to refocus.

5. Do not give the child any feedback during testing. Discuss the answers only after the testing is complete.

6. Always provide positive reinforcements to ensure that the child completes the task. If he or she slows down or wants to give up, provide encouragement and support.

OLSAT® Practice Test for Pre-K and Kindergarten Bright Kids NYC Inc. ©

Bright Kids NYC
OLSAT® Practice Test

Instructions

Pre-K and Kindergarten
Test One

The **Otis-Lennon School Ability Test (OLSAT®)** is a registered trademark of NCS Pearson Inc. Pearson Inc. neither endorses nor supports the content of the OLSAT® Practice Test. All rights reserved. No part of this practice test may be reproduced or transmitted in any form or by any means without written permission from Bright Kids NYC Inc.. ISBN (978-0-9840810-8-0).

Bright Kids NYC Inc. ©

Instructions

Please remember to detach the "Questions for Children" booklet and staple it. Put the booklet in front of the child and instruct him or her to keep the booklet closed until you are both ready to start. If the child is taking the 60-question Kindergarten test, make sure there are at least two sharpened pencils and an eraser ready.

Reminder: **This practice test is designed to simulate an actual OLSAT® test. The administrators of the OLSAT® test are instructed strictly to follow the script. Therefore, it is important for you to follow the script exactly and ask each question only once. The script has been bolded to help differentiate from the rest of the directions.**

OLSAT® Practice Test for Pre-K and Kindergarten

Bright Kids NYC Inc. ©

Part 1

Children in Pre-K will not need to mark their answers. Just ask them to point to the correct answer. For children in Pre-K, replace "mark" with "point" for all the test questions.

Children in Kindergarten will be given the test in a group and will be required to mark their answers properly. Teach them how to bubble in their answers utilizing the sample questions.

SAY: **Today, we are going to do some fun activities in the booklet in front of you. Please keep your booklet closed until I ask you to open it.**

SAMPLE A

SAY: **Now open your booklet and look at the first page. Look at the first question. Here you will see some pictures that go across. When pictures go across, they are said to be in a row.**

SAY: **In this row, you see five animals. One of these animals does not belong with the others. Find the animal that is not like the others.**

Pause while the child looks for the correct animal.

SAY: **Which animal did you find?**

Pause for a response.

SAY: **That is right. The last animal is not like the others. The other animals are all wild animals, but the dog is not a wild animal. The dog is different than all the other animals, isn't it?**

For Pre-K Students Only (skip if your child is in Kindergarten)

Wait for the child to point to the answer.

SAY: **Can you point to the dog? From now on, I will ask you to point to all the answers. However, you can only pick one answer. Can you show me your pointing finger? Great job!**

Check to make sure the child is pointing properly. Tell the child that you will be writing the answer he or she is pointing to. Make sure that the child only points to one answer. If the child starts pointing to different answers, encourage him or her to make a decision. Again, be sure to replace all "mark" with "point" in the script for children taking the 40-question Pre-Kindergarten test.

For Kindergarten Students Only

Wait for the child to answer.

SAY: **Did you find the dog? Mark your answer below the space of the dog. Simply color in the circles completely using the pencil. Try to the fill the circle as best as you can.**

Demonstrate how to fill in an answer if the child seems confused. Remind the child that it does not have to be perfect but circles must be visibly filled. Also let the child know that he or she can bubble only one answer choice. Proceed with Sample B.

SAMPLE B

SAY: **Look at the pictures in this row. One of these pictures does not belong with the others because it is different from the others. Find the picture that is not like the others and mark under the correct picture.**

SAY: **Which picture did you mark?**

Pause for a response.

SAY: **Yes, the third picture is different from the others, isn't it? All of the other pictures have circles at the end of them. You are right. The third picture has both a circle and a square.**

If the child gets the wrong answer:

SAY: **Do you now understand why the third one is different from the other pictures?**

Pause for a response.

SAY: **On the next few pages, we will be doing more activities like these. I will tell you which question and row to work on. Then without my help, you will find the pictures that do not belong with the others and you will mark under the one that does not belong with the others. Do the best that you can with each picture and do not worry if you are not sure of all of the answers.**

SAY: **Now turn the page and look at the first row and the first question.**

SAY:

    1. **Put your finger on the first row. Mark under the picture that does not belong with the other pictures.**

    2. **Put your finger on the second row. Mark under the picture that does not belong with the other pictures.**

    3. **Put your finger on the third row. Mark under the picture that does not belong with the other pictures.**

SAY: **Turn to the next page and look at the first row.**

SAY:

    4. **Put your finger on the first row. Mark under the picture that does not belong with the other pictures.**

    5. **Put your finger on the second row. Mark under the picture that does not belong with the other pictures.**

    6. **Put your finger on the third row. Mark under the picture that does not belong with the other pictures.**

SAY: **Now turn the page and look at the first row.**

SAY:

    7. **Put your finger on the first row. Mark under the picture that does not belong with the other pictures.**

    8. **Put your finger on the second row. Mark under the picture that does not belong with the other pictures.**

9. Put your finger on the third row. Mark under the picture that does not belong with the other pictures.

SAY: **Now turn the page again and look at the first row.**

SAY:

10. Put your finger on the first row. Mark under the picture that does not belong with the other pictures.

11. Put your finger on the second row. Mark under the picture that does not belong with the other pictures.

12. Put your finger on the third row. Mark under the picture that does not belong with the other pictures.

Administer a five minute break. Make sure to tell the child that he or she is not finished and that this is just a brief break.

Part 2

Tell the child that it is time to come back and continue with the activities.

SAMPLE C

SAY: **Now we are going to do a different activity. Look at the first row. Here, you will see four boxes. In the first box on top there is a foot. In the box next to the foot, there is a sock. These top two boxes go together in a certain way. Foot and a sock go together in a certain way. Now look at the first box on the bottom where there is the head of a baby. The other box next to it is empty. Now look at the row of four pictures next to the four boxes and find what should be in the empty box. What do you think goes with a head in the same way that a sock goes with a foot?**

Pause and let the child answer.

SAY: **Did you find the answer?**

SAY: **You are right. The correct answer is the third one, a hat. You wear a sock on your foot and you wear a hat on your head. Great job!**

Make sure the child understands the sample question above before moving on to the next sample question.

SAMPLE D

SAY: **Now point to the second row. Look at the two shapes in the two boxes on the top. These two shapes go together in a certain way. In the first box on top there are two triangles on top of each other. Inside the second box there is only one triangle. Now look at the shape inside the first box on the bottom. There are two half circles on top of each other. What do you think belongs in the empty box? Can you mark under the shape that belongs in the empty box?**

Pause and wait until the child selects an answer.

SAY: **You should have marked the last picture with the half circle. The first picture goes from two triangles on top of each other to one triangle and the two connected half circles should go to a single half circle. The first two are triangles and thus not the right shapes. The third half circle is the wrong color. Do you understand?**

Answer any questions the child may have.

SAY: **Now turn the page and look at the first row.**

Make sure the child is on the first row of the next page.

SAY:

13. **Mark under the picture that goes in the empty box.**

14. **Look at the next row. Mark under the picture that goes in the empty box.**

15. **Look at the last row. Mark under the picture that goes in the empty box.**

SAY: **Turn to the next page and look at the first row.**

SAY:

16. **Mark under the picture that belongs in the empty box.**

17. **Now look at the next row. Mark under the picture that goes in the empty box.**

18. **Now move to the last row. Mark your answer.**

SAY: **Turn the page and look at the first row.**

SAY:

19. **Look at the first row. Mark under the picture that goes in the empty box.**

20. **Now look at the next row. Mark under the picture that goes in the empty box.**

21. **Now move to the last row. Mark your answer.**

SAY: **Turn the page and look at the first row.**

SAY:

22. Mark under the picture that belongs in the empty box.

23. Now look at the next row. Mark under the picture that goes in the empty box.

24. Now move to the last row. Mark your answer.

Give a five minute break as needed. Make sure you tell the child that there will be more exercises to finish once the break is up.

Bright Kids NYC Inc. ©

Part 3

SAMPLE E

SAY: **Open your booklet again. Now we will be working on different types of activities. Look at the first row on top of the page. Now listen very carefully. John wakes up to a type of animal that makes sounds very early to wake him up. Mark under the picture that best describes the type of animal that John wakes up to.**

Pause while the child looks for the correct answer.

SAY: **The first picture is the correct one, right? This picture shows a couple of Roosters. Roosters are animals that wake up early and make crowing. There are no roosters in the other pictures. Do you understand why the first picture is the correct one?**

Pause to see if the child has any questions.

SAMPLE F

SAY: **Now look at the next row. Mark under the picture that shows a big circle between two small triangles. What is the correct answer?**

Pause for a response.

SAY: **The third answer is the correct one. This picture is the only one that has a big circle in between two small triangles.**

Make sure the child understands the example before moving to the next question.

SAMPLE G

SAY: **Go to the next page. Look at the top row. At the beginning of the row, there are pictures in the boxes. These pictures go together in a certain way. Something belongs in the empty box. Look at the answers below. Mark under the picture that belongs in the empty box.**

Pause while the child chooses an answer.

SAY: **The third picture is the correct one. In each box, the tulip stays the same number, but the daisies increase by one. The first box has one tulip and one daisy, the second box has one tulip and two daisies, the third box has one tulip and three daisies, and the fourth box has one tulip and four daisies. Therefore, the empty box should have one tulip and five daisies. Do you understand what we just did?**

Pause for a response. Make sure the child understands the answer before moving to the next question.

SAMPLE H

SAY: **Now look at the last question in the last row. The shapes inside the box go together in a certain way. Look at the answers on the next part of the row. Mark under the shape that belongs in the empty box.**

Pause while the child chooses an answer.

SAY: **The correct answer is the second one, which is the big circle. Let's think about why this is the right answer. In each box, the shape starts big, gets small and then gets big again. The shape remains the same type of shape as well. So in the last row, the big circle is followed by a small circle which then should be followed by a big circle. Do you understand why?**

Pause for a response. If necessary, explain why other answers are wrong if necessary. Make sure your child understands all the sample questions before continuing with the test.

SAY: **On the next pages, we will be doing similar activities. Make sure you listen very carefully since I will only ask the questions once. Then, mark your answer. Are you ready?**

Pause for any questions or concerns the child may have.

SAY: **Now turn the page and look at the first row.**

SAY:

    25. **Listen carefully. When Mike was hungry, his mom offered to buy him his favorite food at the fair. Mike said, "I will go get some ketchup". Mark under the picture that shows what Mike was going to eat.**

26. Now look at the next row. Mark under the pictures that shows this: There is a dotted line in between two solid lines.

27. Now look at the last row. he picture shows six cupcakes. Ava ate two cupcakes and her brother Lucas ate one cupcake. Mark under the picture that shows the number of cupcakes left.

SAY: **Now turn the page again and look at the first row.**

SAY:

28. Listen. Lucia was excited about her new school project. Lucia's teacher asked her to create a collection of items that she can find in a post office and that she can use to mail letters with. Mark under the picture that shows what Lucia probably collected for her school project.

29. Move down to the next row. Mark under the picture that shows this: There is a big dog next to a dog house and a small puppy inside the dog house.

30. Move to the last row. There are pictures in the boxes at the beginning of each row. These pictures go together in a certain way and a picture belongs in the empty box. In the next part of the row, mark under the picture that belongs in the empty box.

SAY: **Now turn your page again and look at the first row.**

SAY:

31. Mark under the picture that shows this: There is exactly one heart above the triangle and two hearts below the triangle.

32. Move to the next row. Look at the four boxes with letters inside them at the beginning of the row. Mark under the picture that shows this:The A and D switch places, and the C and the K remain the same.

33. Move down to the last row. Mark under the picture that shows this: There are two squirrels on top of a tree branch and one on the ground.

Instructions

SAY: **Now turn to the next page and look at the first row.**

SAY:

34. The picture at the beginning of the row shows six cats and three collars. Mark under the picture that shows how many more collars are needed in order for each cat to have exactly one collar.

35. Move to the next row. The shapes in the boxes go together in a certain way and something belongs in the empty box. Mark under the shape that belongs in the empty box.

36. Move down to the last row. There are some birds sitting on a tree branch. Two of the birds fly away. Mark under the picture that shows the number of birds that are left on the branch.

SAY: **Now turn to the next page and look at the first row.**

SAY:

37. Listen. Juan wanted to perform at his school's talent show. He took something to ride on and something to play with. Mark under the picture that shows the items Juan took to the talent show.

38. Move to the next row. Mark under the picture that shows this: The third number is three and the first number is five.

39. Move to the last row. Listen. Mark under the picture that shows this: The arrow that is pointing up is pointing to a black square.

SAY: **Now turn to the next page and look at the first row.**

SAY:

40. Mark under the picture that shows what Juliet and Jane did to cool off on a very hot day

PRE-KINDRERGARTEN CHILDREN STOP HERE

Part 3 (Continued for Kindergarten Children)

Give the child a five-minute break and then continue. Proceed only if the child is in Kindergarten.

SAY: **Now turn the page and look at the first row. Listen carefully.**

SAY:

41. **There are four children at the beginning of the row. Each child ate one cookie and drank a cup of milk. Mark under the picture that shows the total number of cookies and cups of milk they had together.**

42. **Now move to the next row. Look at the boxes at the beginning of the row with pictures inside them. Something belongs in the empty box. In the next part of the row, mark under the picture that belongs in the empty box.**

43. **Move to the last row. Ahmed put his sailboat in between his canoe and his motorboat. Mark under the picture that shows how Ahmed's boats look.**

SAY: **Now turn the page and look at the first row. Listen carefully.**

SAY:

44. **Look at the boxes at the beginning of the row with pictures inside them. Something belongs in the empty box. In the next part of the row, mark under the picture that belongs in the empty box.**

45. **Now move to the next row. Mark under the picture that shows this: There is a dark triangle and a dark circle in between a white triangle and a white circle.**

46. **Move to the last row. Lori's teacher asked the class: "I want each of you to draw two fruits. Make sure you put the page number on the top of your paper." Mark under the picture that shows the paper that is correct.**

SAY: **Now turn the page and look at the first row. Listen carefully.**

SAY:

47. Mark under the picture that shows this: The largest shape in the group is dark. There is only one more large shape that is also dark.

48. Move to the next row. Look at the shapes in the boxes at the beginning of the row. These shapes go together in a certain way. Find the shape that belongs in the empty box and mark under that shape.

49. Move to the last row. Joshua left his favorite treat outside on a hot summer day and it melted. Mark under the picture that shows what Joshua left outside on a hot summer day.

SAY: **Now turn the page and look at the first row. Listen carefully.**

SAY:

50. Look at the shapes in the boxes at the beginning of the row. These shapes go together in a certain way. Find the shape that belongs in the empty box and mark under that shape.

51. Move to the next row. Look at the blocks at the beginning of the row. Listen carefully. Mark under the picture that shows this: Jerry used only three blocks to make a tower and put block three on top of block one and four.

52. Move to the last row. Joanna made a necklace from four beads with numbers on them. She then switched the two and the six and the four and the eight. Mark under the picture that shows Joanna's new necklace.

SAY: **Now turn the page and look at the first row. Listen carefully.**

SAY:

53. Keisha wanted to make a peanut butter sandwich. She was sad when she realized she was missing something sweet that goes well with peanut butter. Mark under the picture of the item Keisha was missing.

54. Move to the next row. Look at the boxes at the beginning of the row with pictures inside them. Something belongs in the empty box. In the next part of the row, mark under the picture that belongs in the empty box.

55. Move to the last row. Adam was excited about his summer vacation. Adam's father promised him that he could catch his own food during his summer vacation. Mark under the picture that best describes what Adam would be doing on his vacation.

SAY: **Now turn the page and look at the first row. Listen carefully.**

SAY:

56. Look at the boxes with shapes as seen at the beginning of the row. Mark under the picture that shows this: The heart moves to the bottom row and the circle moves to the top row. The square stays in the same place.

57. Move to the next row. There are eight flowers as seen at the beginning of the row. Joanna takes three flowers and Jessica takes one. Mark under the picture that shows the flowers that are left.

58. Move to the last row. Mark under the picture that shows this: The largest shape in the picture is a diamond.

SAY: **Now turn the page and look at the first row. Listen carefully.**

SAY:

59. Kelly's mom baked a pizza for a party. Grace, Oliver and Finn had one slice each. Mark under the picture that shows the number of pizza slices left.

60. Move to the last row. Jeremy wanted to build a birdhouse. Jeremy needs something to cut the wood and two different items to paint the wood in order to finish the birdhouse. Mark under the picture that shows the items Jeremy needs to finish the birdhouse.

Answer Key

NUMBER	CORRECT ANSWER	CHILD'S ANSWER	TYPE OF QUESTION
1.	3		Picture Classifications
2.	4		Figural Classifications
3.	3		Picture Classifications
4.	2		Figural Classifications
5.	1		Picture Classifications
6.	2		Figural Classifications
7.	4		Picture Classifications
8.	3		Figural Classifications
9.	5		Picture Classifications
10.	4		Picture Classifications
11.	3		Figural Classifications
12.	4		Picture Classifications
13.	1		Picture Analogies
14.	1		Figural Analogies
15.	4		Figural Analogies
16.	2		Picture Analogies
17.	2		Figural Analogies
18.	2		Figural Analogies
19.	3		Figural Analogies
20.	2		Picture Analogies
21.	1		Figural Analogies
22.	3		Picture Analogies
23.	1		Picture Analogies
24.	3		Figural Analogies
25.	1		Aural Reasoning
26.	2		Aural Reasoning
27.	3		Arithmetic Reasoning
28.	1		Aural Reasoning

Instructions

29.	1		Following Directions
30.	4		Picture Series
31.	3		Following Directions
32.	4		Following Directions
33.	2		Following Directions
34.	1		Arithmetic Reasoning
35.	2		Pattern Matrix
36.	3		Arithmetic Reasoning
37.	1		Aural Reasoning
38.	3		Following Directions
39.	3		Following Directions
40.	1		Aural Reasoning
41.	3		Arithmetic Reasoning
42.	4		Figural Series
43.	3		Following Directions
44.	2		Picture Series
45.	2		Following Directions
46.	4		Following Directions
47.	4		Following Directions
48.	1		Pattern Matrix
49.	3		Aural Reasoning
50.	3		Pattern Matrix
51.	2		Following Directions
52.	1		Following Directions
53.	1		Aural Reasoning
54.	3		Picture Series
55.	1		Aural Reasoning
56.	2		Following Directions
57.	4		Arithmetic Reasoning
58.	4		Following Directions
59.	4		Arithmetic Reasoning
60.	2		Aural Reasoning

OLSAT® Practice Test for Pre-K and Kindergarten   Bright Kids NYC Inc. ©

Bright Kids NYC
OLSAT® Practice Test

Questions for Children

Pre-K and Kindergarten
Test One

The Otis-Lennon School Ability Test (OLSAT®) is a registered trademark of NCS Pearson Inc. Pearson Inc. neither endorses nor supports the content of the OLSAT® Practice Test. All rights reserved. No part of this practice test may be reproduced or transmitted in any form or by any means without written permission from Bright Kids NYC Inc.. ISBN (978-0-9840810-8-0).

OLSAT® Practice Test for Pre-K and Kindergarten

Bright Kids NYC Inc. ©

SAMPLE QUESTIONS

A

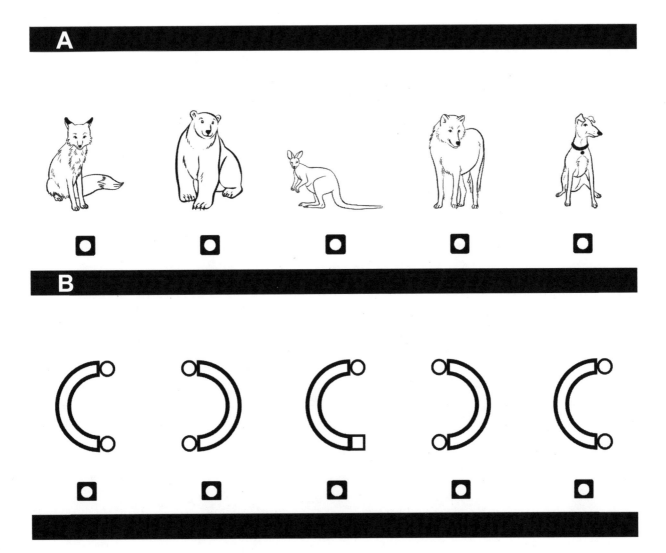

B

Questions for Children

1.

2.

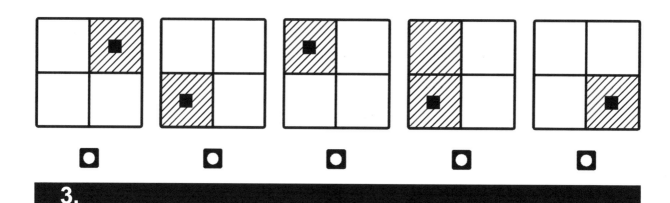

3.

OLSAT® Practice Test for Pre-K and Kindergarten   Bright Kids NYC INC. ©

4.

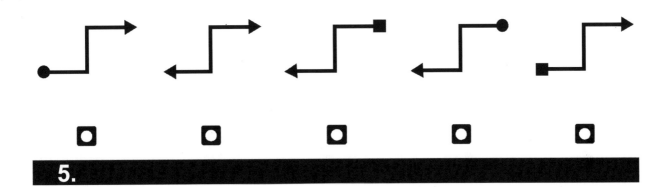

5.

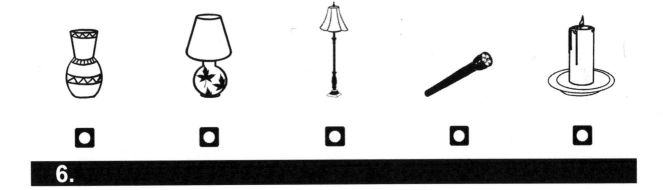

6.

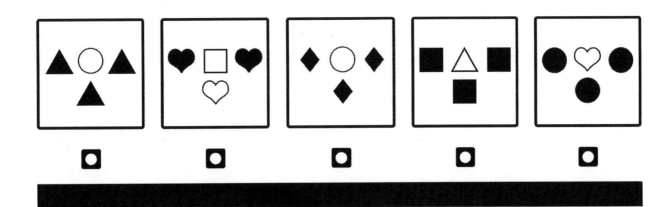

Questions for Children

7.

8.

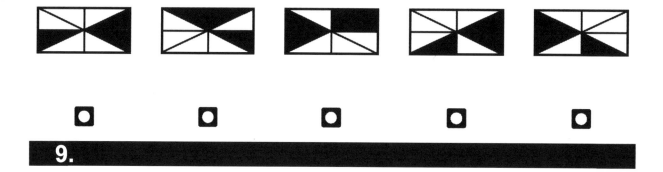

9.

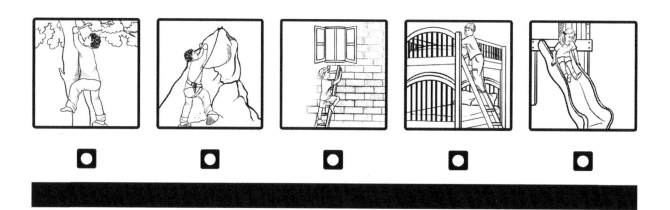

Bright Kids NYC INC. ©

10.

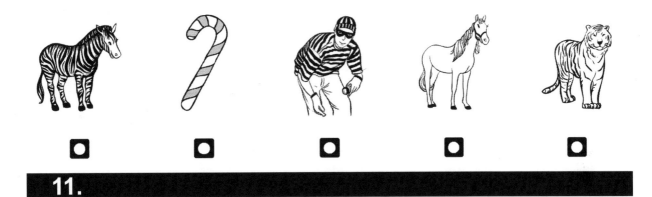

11.

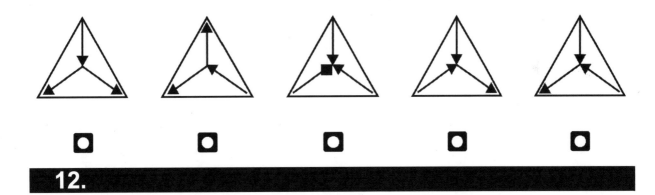

12.

SAMPLE QUESTIONS

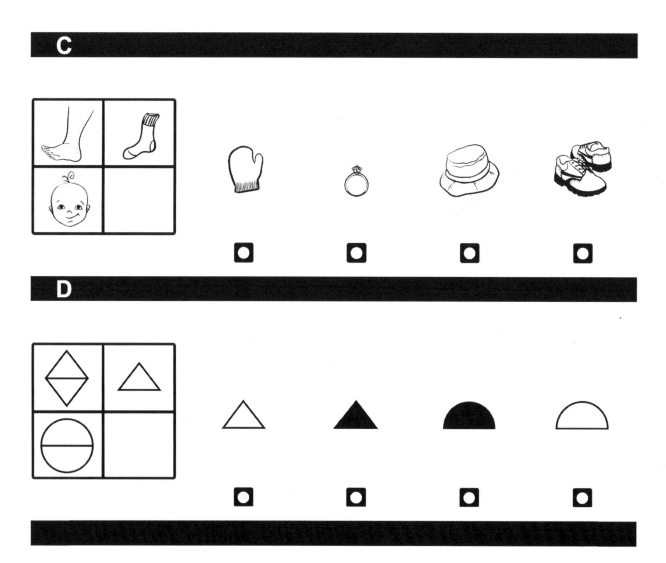

OLSAT® Practice Test for Pre-K and Kindergarten Bright Kids NYC INC. ©

13.

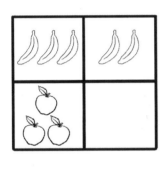

14.

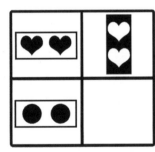

15.

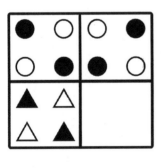
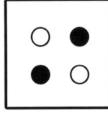

16.

17.

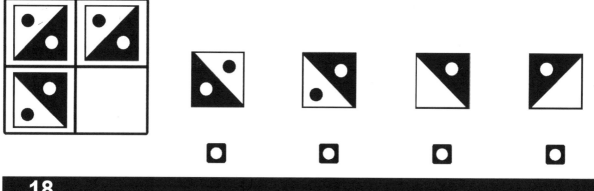

18.

OLSAT® Practice Test for Pre-K and Kindergarten   Bright Kids NYC INC. ©

19.

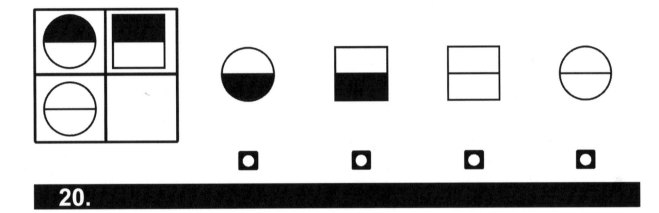

20.

| ☐ | ☐ | ☐ | ☐ |

21.

22.

23.

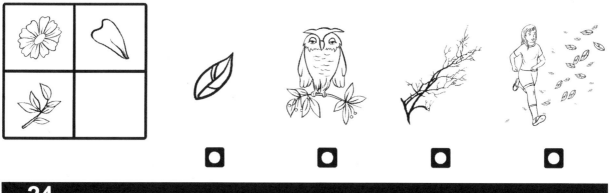

24.

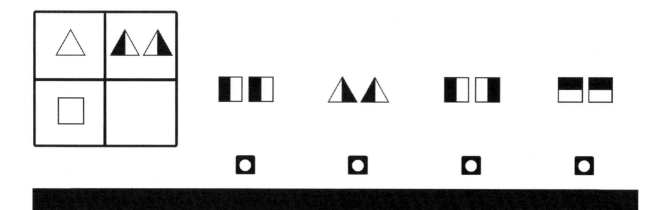

OLSAT® Practice Test for Pre-K and Kindergarten

Bright Kids NYC INC. ©

SAMPLE QUESTIONS

E

F

Questions for Children

G

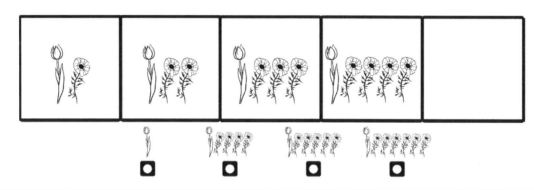

H

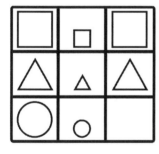

OLSAT® Practice Test for Pre-K and Kindergarten   Bright Kids NYC INC. ©

25.

26.

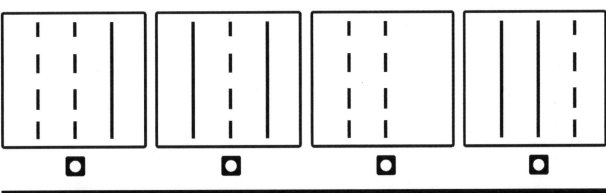

27.

28.

29.

30.

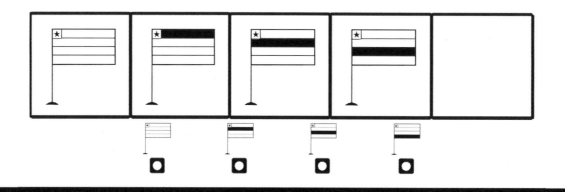

OLSAT® Practice Test for Pre-K and Kindergarten   Bright Kids NYC INC. ©

31.

32.

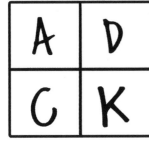 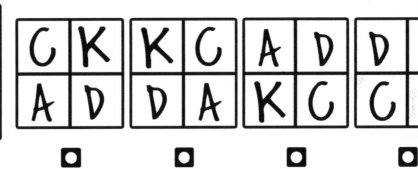

33.

  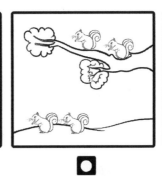 

34.

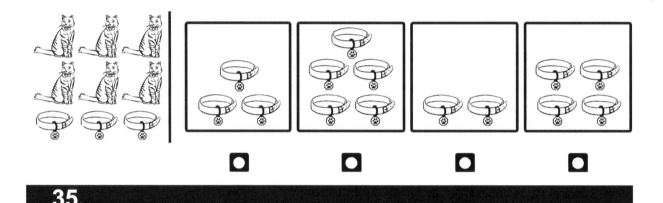

⬜   ⬜   ⬜   ⬜

35.

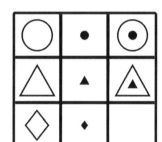

⬜   ⬜   ⬜   ⬜

36.

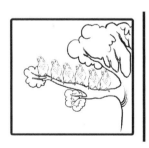            

⬜   ⬜   ⬜   ⬜

37.

38.

| 153 | 351 | 513 | 315 |

39.

 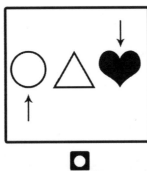 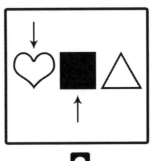 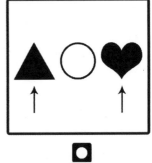

40.

OLSAT® Practice Test for Pre-K and Kindergarten   Bright Kids NYC INC. ©

41.

42.

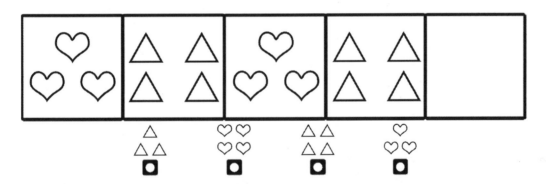

43.

44.

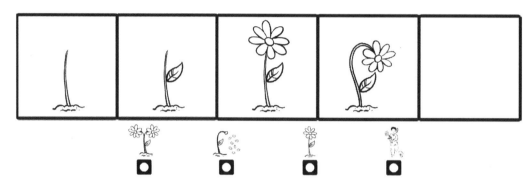

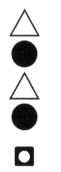  

45.

46.

   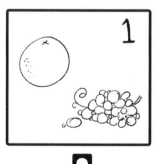

OLSAT® Practice Test for Pre-K and Kindergarten Bright Kids NYC INC. ©

47.

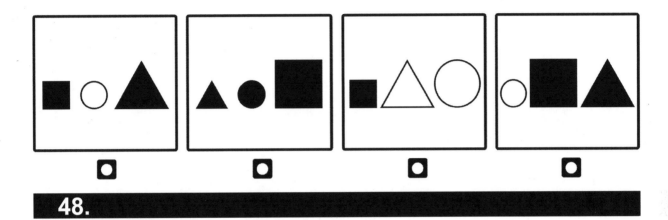

48.

49.

Questions for Children

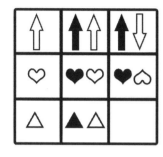

△△   ▲▼   ▲▽   ▽▽

☐   ☐   ☐   ☐

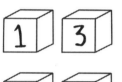

☐   ☐   ☐   ☐

☐   ☐   ☐   ☐

53.

54.

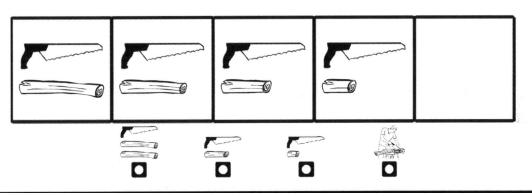

55.

56.

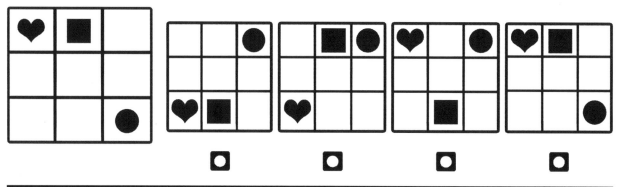

57.

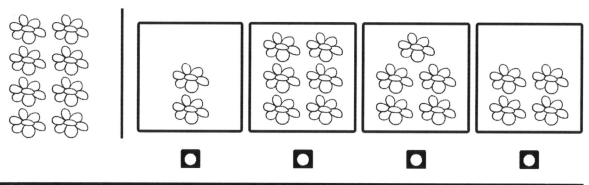

58.

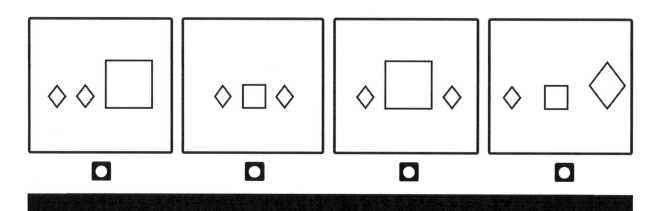

59.

60.

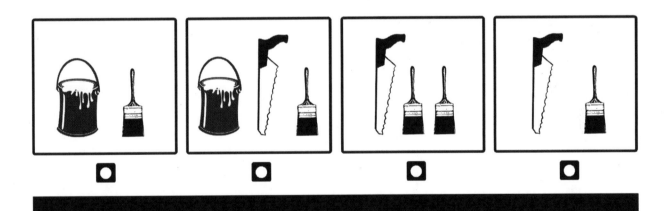